The Strength of Faith

Dedicated to anyone who has been ostracized for being true to yourself. It can get better, but only if you refuse to give up.

Chapter 1

The smell of the bus overwhelmed me when I boarded. All the scents of different perfumes and lack of hygiene were almost more than I could take. The seats were rough and worn. I almost changed my mind, but I found two vacant seats in the back and quickly occupied one of them. I silently hoped that I didn't end up sharing the space with someone else. It was going to be a long painful ride and I wanted to be alone to work things out in my head. That hope was quickly dashed.

"Is anyone sitting here?" the woman asked.

"No," I responded, keeping my eyes focused on some imaginary object outside the window.

"Where ya headin'?"

Her Georgia drawl was unmistakable when she spoke.

"California," I whispered without interest in a long conversation.

I assumed she detected my disinterest. She placed her bag on the floor between us and quietly made herself comfortable.

The bus pulled out of the terminal with a jolt and soon we were on the highway. I watched the scenery fly by the window. The thoughts in my head were moving just as fast as the trees on the side of the road. The dark storm clouds matched my mood. I couldn't erase the earlier events from my memory, as much as I wanted them to go away.

***

"Faith, can you come down here. Your mother and I need to talk with you about something important before you head out to the library."

My father's voice boomed from the bottom of the stairs. He was an intimidating man, even without trying. My little sister and I were always slightly afraid of him, even though he had never done anything to physically harm us.

"Be there in a sec," I called back from my bedroom.

I finished brushing my hair, threw all of my things for the study session in a bag, and headed downstairs. I couldn't imagine what they wanted. My parents rarely wanted to talk to either my sister or me. They weren't the nurturing type or the kind that was interested in the daily lives of their kids.

Both of my parents were sitting at the table in the kitchen waiting on me. I sat down, poured a glass of orange juice. I guessed that they were having a dinner party or something and needed Cassie and I to be our darling little selves. I braced myself for the usual speech that we got before one of their events.

"Who is Randi?" my father asked immediately.

His question threw me off just bit. The glass of juice was shaking in my hand. I decided it was best if I just put it down.

"A friend from school. I've told you about her. Why?"

"How close are you two?" my mother asked.

"Pretty close, I guess."

I wasn't sure where this was going, but my nerves were on edge. My palms were beginning to sweat and I tried to dry them on my jeans.

My father pulled a stack of papers out from under the daily newspaper and laid them down in front of me. I couldn't hide the shock when I saw what they were.

"What are you doing with my e-mails?" I asked defensively.

My father refused to acknowledge the question or the fact that he had invaded my privacy and read my personal letters.

"What exactly is the nature of your relationship with this girl?" he asked as if he was a detective interrogating a suspect.

I could feel the hairs on the back of my neck stand up as I grew angry. I couldn't believe what I was seeing on the table. Every e-mail that I had ever exchanged with Randi was in front of me in black and white. I guess it was my fault for not deleting them, but I had kept them so that I could go back and read them when I was missing her.

"You have no right going through my things. Those are personal. I'm an adult and should have some reasonable expectation of privacy."

"Not as long as you still live under our roof," my mother interjected. "Faith, we haven't raised you like that. You know that a relationship like that is wrong. It has to stop before it goes too far."

My head was spinning out of control. The shock of what was playing out was overwhelming. It was if I was living a nightmare. I knew where the conversation was going and I couldn't stop it. The tears were welling up in my eyes, but I fought them back. I wasn't going to break down in front of them.

"It hasn't gone too far, has it?" she asked.

Both of my parents were sitting across from me, glaring. Their eyes on me felt like daggers piercing my skin.

"What do you think is too far?" I asked angrily.

"Have you had sex with her?" my father interjected.

My father's blunt question startled me and I felt the heat rise in my face. There was no good way to answer him. If I said no, they would know I was lying. If I admitted to it, things were going to only get worse.

I took a deep breath and tried to steady my nerves before I finally answered them.

"I don't think it is any of your business if I'm sleeping with her or anyone else."

'Oh God!" my mother exclaimed and got up from the table.

She was always so overly dramatic when things didn't go the way that she thought they should. She was leaning on the counter by the sink and pretending to sob as if her heart had been ripped from her. It was an act that she had perfected over the years.

"I was afraid of that," she said after what she thought was an appropriate pause. "You are going to see Dr. Raymond. His office is only a few blocks from campus and your appointment is at 2:30 tomorrow afternoon. You will have plenty of time to get there after your last class."

"Who is Dr. Raymond, and why do I have an appointment with him?"

"He's a therapist who specializes in your condition. He can help you, Faith." My father said, taking control of the conversation.

"My condition?"

There was no way that I could contain my emotions at that point. I knew before it happened that I was about to say things that I shouldn't, but I was so infuriated that I had no control.

"I can't believe this," I yelled. "There is nothing wrong with me and I am not going to some whack job that thinks he can cure me. I'm gay. It's as simple as that. I don't have some disease. There isn't a pill for it. It's who I am and you need to deal with it."

I pushed away from the table and stood up with such force that the chair fell over behind me and the glass of juice spilled on the table. I was shaking with anger and fighting harder to hold back those tears. My father had also stood up and walked over to me. He gripped my arms so tightly that it hurt. My mother was cleaning up the spilled juice as if nothing else was going on in the room.

"You need help, Faith," he tried to sound concerned. "Give Dr. Raymond a chance."

"You've lost your damn minds if you think I am going to this so-called doctor."

"You don't have a choice," my mother said casually as she rinsed the cloth in the sink.

"Like hell I don't!"

I felt the sting of my father's hand on my cheek as soon as the words had come from within me. I had lost my battle with the tears. They flowed down my cheeks uncontrollably.

"You can both go to hell!" I screamed at them and ran out of the house.

I had no idea where I was going when I drove off, but I knew I couldn't spend another moment with them in that house. I spent a couple hours at the park thinking and then I made my decision. I went back to the house after both of them had left and got a few clothes and other necessities. I got cash from the ATM and headed to the bus station.

***

"You want to talk about it?" the woman asked.

I wiped the tears from my eyes and shook my head. I had no idea who this woman was and really didn't feel like spilling my guts to anyone. I figured she would feel the same way as my parents and I didn't need another person passing judgment on me for something they have no clue about.

"You know, everyone has a story. Sometimes it helps to share it. My name's TJ. If you decide you want to talk, I'm here. It's a long ride and we might as well get to know each other since we are stuck together."

She settled back in the seat and pulled a book from her bag. I finally took a long look at her. She was older, probably the age of my parents. Her short brown hair was streaked with silver and there were definite lines around her eyes. She wore no make-up and was dressed very simple. Her hands were rough looking, but her voice had been very gentle when she was speaking to me.

"Faith," I said softly.

"Pardon?" she asked, looking up from her book.

"My name's Faith."

"It's nice to meet you, Faith. So, what's taking you all the way to Cali? Are you visiting family?"

"No," I said with a sigh. "I'm moving out there."

"Really? I don't mean to offend you, but you look awfully young to be on your own."

"No offense taken. I'm eighteen."

"Are you going to school out there?" TJ asked me.

"No," I said, fighting back the tears again.

"I left for Cali when I was about your age." TJ said. "I had big dreams of being in show business. I wanted to be a screen writer."

"Really?"

"Yeah," she laughed. "It didn't work out though. I manage a bookstore now."

"At least you went after your dream," I said. "If you live in California, what are you doing on a bus from Georgia?"

"Ah! You want to know my story," she said with a smile. "I'll make a deal with you. I'll tell ya mine and you share a little of yours. How's that?"

Her smile was warm and genuine and it made me loosen up a little.

"Okay," I agreed.

"My mom died when I was really young so I barely remember her. My dad never remarried, so it was just the two of us. He was a terrible father, to say the least. He stayed drunk, wouldn't hold down a job, and gambled away what little money we had. He abused me mentally, physically, and sexually. I think he blamed me for my mom's death. The abuse didn't stop until I was about your age."

"What happened then?" I asked.

She took a long pause before she spoke again.

"In short, I told my dad I was gay, he beat the hell out of me, and I hopped on a bus just like this one. I didn't really have anywhere to go so I got as far away as I could. Like I said before, I wanted to write. California seemed to be my best choice. I worked a lot of odd jobs before I realized that I wasn't getting anywhere with the writing thing. I finally gave up on that dream and took a job in a local bookstore. It paid the bills and I eventually worked my way up to manager."

"Did you and your dad ever work out your differences?"

"Not even close. I heard last week that he had passed away. I came back here just to make sure."

I didn't know what to say. I just looked at TJ, trying to absorb what she had just confessed to me. I thought I had it bad, but at least I had been raised by both parents and wasn't abused.

"Your turn," she finally said to me.

I relayed the events of the morning to her and she listened intently. I broke down several times and she tried to comfort me. I actually did feel better after I had talked a little bit about what had happened.

"So why are you heading out west?" she asked. "Do you have more family there?"

"Randi, my girlfriend, is there. She was offered an internship at a studio and left a few months ago. She's taking classes and working on some movie set. She'll actually graduate at the end of the semester. She plans on staying if she can find a permanent job, and I had planned on joining her later. I'm just going sooner than either of us planned."

"You don't think your parents will cool down and things will be okay if you stay?"

"They don't cool down. Once they get on something, it's for good."

"Was Randi excited when you told her you were coming?" TJ asked.

"I haven't told her yet. I'm going to surprise her."

"I bet she'll like that surprise."

My cell phone rang and I pulled it out of my bag. I couldn't answer it. It was Cassie and I had no idea how to begin to talk to her about what had happened that morning.

"Your parents?" TJ asked.

"My little sister, Cassie. I know I need to talk to her, but I don't know what to say. I can only imagine what Mom and Dad have already told her. I think I'll wait to call her when I get settled."

"Are you two very close?"

"I've taken care of her for the last five years. Our parents are always gone and it's really just the two of us. Dad's always working or playing golf, and Mom has her groups that she belongs to. That doesn't leave a lot of time for us. They have us around when they need to look like adoring parents. It's all for show."

"You should at least let her know you're okay." TJ suggested. "How old is she?"

"She's fifteen."

TJ's demeanor had put me at ease on the bus ride, which was much longer than I expected. We talked about so many different things and I took several naps during the trip. I hadn't realized that busses made so many stops and had such long layovers. Forty-eight hours later I stepped off the bus in California. I was scared to death, but ready to begin a new life.

TJ pulled out her wallet and handed me a card while we were saying good-bye in the bus station.

"If you need anything or just want to talk, call me. My personal number is on the card. That other number is a center for gay teens that I help run. You might want to come by sometime. We have some pretty cool events and you might meet some new friends."

"I'll keep that in mind," I told her as I stuck the card in my bag.

I watched TJ and her girlfriend walk out of the bus terminal and it made me want to see Randi even more. They looked like the perfect couple, walking hand in hand and talking to each other. I dialed Randi's number and listened to the ringing on the other end. I was about to hang up when she finally answered.

"Hey," I said into the phone.

"Faith! This is a surprise. What's up?"

"I need your address. I have a surprise for you, but I have no idea where to send it."

Randi gave me the address without any hesitation. I knew that she never expected me to be the surprise. All I had to do was find a taxi and I would be one step closer to feeling safe in her arms. I was so nervous and excited that it was hard for me to concentrate.

There were several taxis waiting outside the terminal and I hopped in one and handed the driver the piece of paper with the address. He took off into traffic, scaring me a bit with his erratic driving.

I tried to see some of the sights as we flew through the streets, but it was hopeless. I kept seeing Randi in my mind, imagining her happiness when she would open the door and see me standing there.

Fifteen minutes later, I was standing in front of her apartment building. I have no idea why I was so nervous, but I was shaking like a leaf as I walked in the high-rise apartment building. I found her apartment number and knocked on the door.

"Can I help you?" the auburn-haired woman asked when she opened the door.

I stared at her without speaking because she answered the door wearing only a t-shirt. I was finally able to speak when she asked if she could help me the second time.

"I'm sorry. I think I have the wrong apartment," I said.

"Is that the takeout?" the voice called from behind her. I recognized it instantly as Randi.

"Randi?" I asked, trying to look around the other woman.

When the woman stepped to the side, I saw Randi standing there wrapped in only a towel.

"Faith?" Randi said, obviously in shock. "What are you doing here?"

"I told you I had a surprise for you. I guess I got the surprise, didn't I?" I whispered.

I ran for several blocks before I stopped. My sides were hurting and I struggled to breathe. My bag was cutting into my shoulders and tears were clouding my vision. My phone was ringing in my pocket. I saw that it was Randi, but I couldn't stand the thought of hearing her voice. I turned it off and leaned up against a building.

When I could finally breathe without the feeling that my heart would explode, I continued walking. I knew nothing about Los Angeles, so I was completely lost. The sights and sounds temporarily took my mind off of my troubles. I was amazed by the town itself. I understood why people wanted to move there. It was so busy and you could easily get absorbed by the crowd of people and become invisible. That was exactly what I wanted to do at that very moment.

Hours had passed and the day turned to night. I felt a chill in the air. I was going to have to find a place to stay for the night and figure out what to do next. I couldn't believe how my world had turned upside down in only two days.

The flashing lights of a diner caught my attention. I realized that I had not eaten very much since I left home and thought it might be a good idea to get some nourishment in me. I found a small table in the back away from everyone and sat down. The diner was noisy and crowded. The sounds of plates banging together and the roar of jumbled voices were actually calming me as I looked over the menu.

"What can I get you to drink?" the female voice asked.

"Coffee," I said softly, not taking my eyes off the menu.

She placed the coffee cup in front of me and I ordered a cheeseburger and fries. The coffee was so strong that I could hardly get enough cream and sugar in it. I sipped on it and watched the people interacting with each other until my burger was brought to my table.

I tried to eat, but my stomach was tied in knots. I was playing with my fries, pushing them around on my plate when the waitress came back to check on me.

"Something wrong with your food?" she asked.

"The food's fine," I told her. "I guess I just wasn't as hungry as I thought."

"Where are you from?" she asked.

I finally looked up at her. Hers was the first face that I had really focused on since the incident at Randi's. She was an older woman, probably in her forties. Her long black hair was streaked with silver and pulled back in a ponytail. Her eyes were dark and appeared tired. I thought that she had probably been gorgeous when she was younger, but years had taken a toll on her looks.

"Georgia." I quietly answered.

"That's pretty far away. Are you on vacation?"

"I wish," I said averting my eyes from her again. I didn't want to cry any more, but I could feel it building up inside of me.

"Are you all right?"

The concern in her voice sounded genuine and her hand on my shoulder was gentle, but I really didn't want to spill my guts to another complete stranger.

"I will be." I cleared my throat and finished my coffee.

"If you need anything else, just let me know. Okay?"

She had started to walk away when I spoke again.

"You wouldn't happen to know a reasonable hotel close by, would you?"

"As a matter of fact, I do," she said turning back to me. "My boyfriend is the night manager at the Regency. It's isn't that fancy, but it's clean and cheap. Let me write down the directions for you."

She left for just a moment and retuned with detailed directions to the hotel.

"His name is Mike. When you get there, tell him that Maria sent you. Are you sure you're okay?"

"Just tired," I managed. "I just need a good night's sleep."

I paid the bill and slowly followed the directions to the hotel. It would be so good to be able to relax in a bed.

***

Maria had been right about one thing. It wasn't the greatest place to stay, but at least I could shower and try to get a little sleep. I turned my phone on and dumped my bag on the bed. I realized at that moment just how little I had brought with me. My phone vibrated and beeped as all of the messages came through. Like it or not, I was going to have to clear them.

After reading the texts and listening to the voicemails, I dialed one of the numbers that I had been avoiding. My heart almost broke when I heard Cassie's voice on the other end.

"Are you alone?" I asked.

"Of course I am. It's one in the morning. Where are you?"

"I don't want to tell you right now, Cass. If you don't know, they can't force you to tell them."

"Okay. Can you at least tell me what happened the other day and why you haven't called me before now? I have been worried sick about you, Faith."

I could hear her voice cracking on the other end. I hated myself for leaving her without a word, but I didn't see any other way.

"I haven't called because I've been trying to wrap my head around everything and get myself together. I've also been on the road. Other than being exhausted, I'm physically okay. What did Mom and Dad tell you?"

"They haven't told me anything other than you got mad and left. What happened?"

"It's a long story. I will tell you that they know about Randi now."

"That's kind of what I thought. Are you still here in town?"

"No. I'm in another state. Tell Mom and Dad that they need to go get my car. I left it in that shopping center over by the bus station. They'll need to take the spare keys. I put my set of keys in the glove box and locked it."

"Do you have money? Where are you staying? You aren't on the street, are you?"

"Cass!" I interrupted her. "I have money. I cleaned out my bank account before I left. I also have a credit card that they don't know about, and I'm not on the street. I'm actually in a comfy hotel room. Now, I'm going to hang up and get some sleep. You should do the same. You have school tomorrow. I'll call you again in a few days."

I hated hanging up on my sister because I worried about her being alone. She depended on me for so much. I couldn't dwell on that though. I had other problems to contend with.

I could only listen to a few of Randi's messages before I started deleting them. Once they were gone, I showered and crawled into bed. It was only midnight, but my body was still on east coast time.

As tired as I was, I only drifted in and out of sleep. In one of my semi-conscious states, I answered my ringing phone. Randi's voice caused me to sit straight up in bed.

"It's about time you answered. I've left you tons of messages, hoping you would call back."

"I don't want to talk to you right now," I told her as I choked back tears. "I have a ton of things on my mind that I have to sort out. You really blew me away today."

"Faith, what you saw today wasn't what you're thinking it was. Can we meet somewhere and talk?"

"I'm mentally and physically exhausted, Randi. Maybe some other time, after I've had time to get things together."

"Breakfast tomorrow? I will meet you anywhere you want."

I thought about it for a moment. A little voice inside of me told me not to agree, but my heart overruled it.

"Okay. Breakfast it is. There is a little diner that I found today. It's in a storefront. I'm not sure what street it's on, but the name is Tony's. It can't be too far from your place because I walked there. Meet me there at eight in the morning. I'll only have a few minutes because I've got a lot to do."

"I'll be there," she said.

There was a brief silence between the two of us.

"Faith, I love you."

"I'll see you in the morning, Randi."

I wanted to say it back to her, but I couldn't. I was confused and hurt. What could possibly be different about what I saw in her apartment? It seemed pretty obvious to me what was going on there.

Chapter 2

The diner was packed and Randi wasn't there when I arrived. I found a booth and ordered coffee, bacon, eggs, and toast. I flipped through a newspaper to the classifieds while I drank my coffee. There were quite a few jobs listed, but not many that I was qualified for. I made a few notes and put the paper away when I my food came. I looked at my watch. It was eight and Randi still hadn't arrived.

When the waitress came by to pick up my plate, I asked for the check. I was just about to leave when I saw her walk through the door. My heart ached at the sight of her.

Her long blonde hair was pulled up into a ponytail and swinging from side to side. Her jeans and t-shirt hung loose on her small body. She was tomboyish, but to me she was the most beautiful girl on the planet.

"Sorry I'm late," she said, trying to kiss me. "Traffic was terrible."

I turned my head slightly and her warm lips touched my cheek. I was sitting close to the edge of the seat so that she couldn't sit beside me. My defenses were weakening, even though I was trying to keep them strong. I knew it wouldn't take much convincing from her to get me back in her good graces. Then I thought about what I had seen the night before. I was instantly furious again.

"I never expected to see you here," Randi said.

"Obviously," I replied sarcastically, keeping my eyes on my half empty coffee cup.

"What's going on? Why are you out here?"

"It's a long story," I said as I physically forced the lump back down in my throat.

"I've got time. I've missed you so much."

Randi reached across the table and touched my hand. Her skin was so warm and soft. I thought about the times that she had held me closely.

"I left home. Things happened and I had no other choice. I thought I could come out here and we could be together. I guess that was stupid of me, huh?"

"Faith, you got the wrong idea yesterday."

"Really? You had another woman in your apartment and both of you were barely dressed. I think it's pretty obvious what I interrupted."

The hurt had been completely replaced by anger. I could feel the heat as my face reddened. I wanted to scream, but had to keep my composure in the diner.

"That isn't my apartment," she said. "It belongs to the studio. Brittany's another intern and we were placed together as roommates. We had both just gotten home from work and had ordered food. I was grimy from work and had to take a shower before the take out arrived. I was just getting out when you knocked. That's all. I swear to you. I love you, Faith. That hasn't changed."

I finally looked into her eyes. There was a sadness and pleading that I had never seen before. My heart melted and the anger flowed out of my body as quickly as it had come. I wanted to feel the welcoming embrace that I had expected when I got off that bus.

"I feel really stupid right now," I whispered. "I guess after the last couple of days, I did jump to the wrong conclusions. I'm so sorry, Randi. Can you forgive me?"

She took both of my hands in hers and squeezed them tightly.

"It's okay, babe. I would have probably thought the same thing. So tell me what all has happened."

The tears flowed and I told her everything that had happened. We probably sat in that booth for three hours. She couldn't believe that I had left so suddenly, much less that I traveled across the country to be with her.

"Where did you stay last night?" she asked once I had finished.

"A hotel down the street called the Regency. A waitress that was here last night recommended it. It isn't the greatest, but it'll do for now. I was hoping to be able to stay with you once I got here. I guess I should have realized that they would put you up in a place. I just wasn't thinking clearly when everything went down."

"I wish you could stay with me, but the studio won't allow it. That was one of the many rules they gave us when we moved into the place."

"It's okay," I told her. "I have money to get me by for a while. I can stay at the hotel until I find a job. I'll be okay. I just have a lot to do to get settled. Again, I didn't thoroughly think things through."

"Your impulsiveness is one of the things that I love about you," Randi laughed. "I have an idea. I have to work this afternoon and things will probably run late. Why don't we make plans for tomorrow to do something? I don't have class in the morning so I can take you around town and show you where the studio is. I can't take you in because they won't allow interns to have guests, but you can at least see it. We can grab some lunch at a fabulous place that I know. I just have to be back in time to work in the afternoon."

My heart skipped a beat and I agreed quickly. It would be wonderful to spend the day with Randi. I had missed her so much since she had left.

***

My phone was ringing as I unlocked the hotel room. I dropped my things on the bed and looked at it. It was TJ's number.

"Hello?"

"Faith, I just wanted to check on you and see how things were going," TJ said.

"It's been a pretty rough day," I confessed. "I've been out all day looking for a job with no luck. There wasn't anything in the classifieds, so I just hit the streets in the neighborhood where I am staying. The places that I'm qualified to work aren't hiring. It's frustrating."

"Where are you staying?"

"The Regency," I told her. "It's a cheap hotel that was recommended to me last night."

"What about Randi?" she asked.

I told her everything that had happened.

"Maybe things will work out and you won't have to stay in that hotel long. There's another reason that I called. I want you to come to the center this evening. Pam and I will come by and pick you up. I want you to meet some people."

"I'm really kind of tired," I protested.

"We won't keep you out long. It'll be fun. Be ready in about an hour."

Resisting was useless. TJ wouldn't give up until I agreed.

***

Several younger teens ran up to TJ and Pam and hugged them when we walked into the center. I couldn't hear anything that was said because of the loud thumping music. The lights were flashing with the beat of the bass. It was almost a night club atmosphere. TJ took my hand and led me through the crowd of people into a much quieter office in the back.

"Dale? You got a minute?"

The young man behind the desk looked up from the file in front of him.

"Of course I do," he said standing and walking from behind his desk.

He hugged TJ and asked who I was.

"This is Faith," she told him. "She's the one I told you about that I met coming back home."

"Hi Faith," he said to me, extending his hand. "I'm Dale."

"She really needs a job," TJ answered. "She was out all day today looking and didn't have any luck. It's hard when you don't know the area. You think you might be able to help her out?"

"Leave her here with me for a few minutes and I'll see what I can do. I may have a couple of leads for her."

TJ closed the door behind her, leaving me alone in the office with Dale. I had no idea what was going on, but obviously Dale was used to TJ just dropping people off and leaving.

He appeared to be slightly younger than TJ. He had wavy brown hair that was a little unkempt. His large green eyes gave his face the appearance of innocence.

"What do you think of the center?" he asked.

"It seems pretty nice. It looks like there are quite a few people that come here."

"There are always more when we have events likes this, but we have a large number of regulars that we provide different kinds of assistance to as they need it. It's also a safe place for them to just hang out. What kind of job are you looking for?"

"Anything," I told him. "I just need some income. I came to town with a little money, but I know it won't last long."

"Do you have any work experience at all?"

"I was working in the admissions office at school until I left. I answered the phones, scheduled appointments, made copies, filed, and anything else that they needed me to do."

"I think I might have the perfect job for you," he said pulling a card from his desk drawer. "This lady doesn't usually hire through me, but she is a personal friend and she needs an assistant. It'll be doing almost the same type thing. It isn't the greatest pay, but it is a little better than most of the fast food places around here. Her name is Michelle. Call her in the morning and tell her that I referred you."

He handed me the card along with an envelope that he had pulled out along with it.

"What's this?" I asked opening the envelope.

"It's just a little something to help you out while you get on your feet."

I was shocked to see the four one hundred dollar bills inside.

"I didn't come in here for money," I said, trying to hand it back to him.

"Keep it. You might need it. You will need clothes for work, maybe even need a little help with living expenses until you get going good. It's what we do here when we can. We have people that make donations for this purpose. Is there anything else that we can help you with? Do you need someone to talk to, maybe to vent a little?"

I had to choke back the tears. I couldn't believe that there were people that actually cared and tried to help others. It just wasn't what I was used to seeing.

"No. I'm dealing with everything pretty well. TJ let me vent on the bus ride. That helped a lot."

"If you ever change your mind, we have peer counselors and a few professional counselors that volunteer. Don't be afraid to ask."

"I'll keep that in mind," I said with a grin.

"Now, go have fun," he told me with a huge toothy smile.

When I found TJ she was talking with a beautiful olive-skinned young woman.

"Did he have something?" she asked.

"He gave me a lead that I'm going to follow up on in the morning. It sounds promising,"

"Good. Now you can take your mind off things for a bit. This is Marissa, our in-house DJ," she said pointing at the young woman. "She has volunteered to make sure that you forget all of your problems tonight."

"Really?" I asked with a slight laugh.

"First of all, everyone calls me Rissa."

Her smile was bright and lit up her entire face. Her long black hair was pulled back behind her shoulders and showed off her beautiful features. I had never seen anyone that gorgeous who wasn't on television or in a magazine.

"Let's leave these old folks alone before they try to get us into trouble. I'll introduce you to the cool people," she said taking my hand and leading me away from TJ and Pam.

I tagged along like a child behind her as she guided me through the center. We talked with a few people before she had to go change the music. I went with her to the table where her equipment was set up and watched as she worked.

I was enjoying myself and time was passing so quickly. I honestly wasn't ready to leave when TJ found me again.

"TJ, I can take Faith home if she isn't ready to leave now," Rissa volunteered. "I promise she'll be safe with me."

There was a little teasing between the two, but I ignored it. It was almost as if TJ was trying to set me up with Rissa, but I wasn't interested in anything more than friendship.

"Where do you live?" Rissa asked while we were packing her equipment into her car.

"I'm staying at the Regency for now. I hope this job pans out and I can find an apartment soon."

"Well at least you aren't on the street. Trust me, that's no fun."

I stared at Rissa and wondered what her story was. If she wanted me to know, she would tell me.

Her little black sports car made its way easily through the crowded streets. It wasn't long before I started recognizing the area and I knew we would soon be at our destination.

"You want to grab a bite to eat before I take you home?" she asked.

It wasn't hard for me to agree. She was so easy to talk to and I was enjoying her company. We talked for another couple of hours over cheeseburgers and fries at Tony's. I told her how I ended up there and waited for her to volunteer her information, but she never did.

It was getting late and I decided to walk back to the hotel, since it was only a few blocks. Rissa and I exchanged phone numbers and agreed to hang out sometime. I really liked her. She seemed down to earth and wise way beyond her years. She kind of intrigued me.

Chapter 3

Randi's phone rang and rang. Finally I left her a voicemail.

"Randi, I won't be able to make it today. Someone gave me a lead on a job and I have an interview this morning. Not sure how long it will take, but I'll call you when I'm done. I love you."

Those three words came out just as easily as they had before. I felt so ashamed of myself for jumping to the conclusions that I had before. If I had thought it through, I would have known that Randi loved me and was faithful to me.

I stepped out of the cab and looked up at the building in amazement. I had never seen anything like it. Its mirrored windows reflected the sun light and made it look like it was on fire. The inside of the building was just as beautiful. The marble floors and the gorgeous art work that decorated the walls definitely gave the appearance of success.

Michelle appeared as soon as the receptionist paged her. She took me into her office and got down to business quickly.

"So you're Faith. Dale called me last night and told me about you. I don't usually hire people through Dale, but he assured me that I would be pleased with you. Did he tell you about the job?"

"He told me it was a position for an assistant and it was similar to what I've done before."

"I love your accent," she said, leaning back in her chair. "Where are you from?"

"Georgia," I answered with a little self-consciousness.

"People are going to love to hear you talk. It is so unique," she told me. "So tell me about your last job."

I told her about my duties on campus, which led to the question I dreaded.

"Why did you leave that job?" she asked seriously.

I could feel my pulse quicken and my mind raced right along with it. I wondered what Dale had told her. I wasn't sure exactly what he knew about me. I nervously smoothed the wrinkles out of my skirt.

"I decided to move here," I finally replied.

"Faith, I'll be honest with you. The main reason I don't usually hire through Dale is lack of stability. A lot of people that he deals with come and go on a whim. I need someone who is going to be here. Tell me honestly, are you going to stick around or are you going to realize in a few weeks or months that you need to go back home?"

"I'm going to stay."

I forced the words out of my mouth and hoped that they sounded convincing. Obviously they did.

I was probably in the interview for two hours. When I left, I almost floated out of the building. I was starting my new job the next day. I couldn't wait to tell everyone.

I pulled out my phone and started dialing Randi's number. I changed my mind and decided to surprise her. I picked up some takeout and headed to her apartment. I thought we could at least have some lunch together before she went to work.

"Is Randi home?" I asked when Brittany opened the door.

"No," she said. "Come on in for a minute though."

I stepped inside and set the bag down on a table by the door.

"Have a seat, Faith."

I took my first long look at her. She was at least in her thirties, but still very attractive. I nervously sat down on the edge of the sofa and watched her as she sat on the chair across from me.

"Why are you here?" she asked.

"I picked up some lunch for Randi and me. I thought that we…"

"I don't mean today," she interrupted. "Why did you follow her here to California?"

"I didn't follow her here. I came here to…I don't have to explain myself to you. Randi's my girlfriend. That's between us."

I was angry again, but this time not at Randi. My fury was directed at this woman who was getting into my business and she didn't belong there. I wondered what right she thought she had in questioning me about what I was doing.

"Faith, she told me that you didn't take the break up well when she left. It's time to move on. She has."

I stared at her in disbelief. The room was starting to spin and I tried to focus on Brittany as she talked. Her voice seemed far away.

"She came out here to be with me, Faith. It's over between you two."

I just stared at her for what seemed like forever and let the questions stream through my mind. Had Randi lied to me to string me along? Was this woman telling me the truth? Was Brittany some kind of psycho that thought she had a relationship with Randi? I didn't know what to believe. I was confused when I left that apartment.

Once I got back to the hotel room, I collapsed on the bed in tears with those same questions still repeating over and over in my head. Why would Randi lie to me about it? She was so convincing at the diner. Why couldn't I see through her if she had been lying to me? I cried myself to sleep and didn't wake up until my phone rang several hours later.

It was Randi, and I refused to answer it. I didn't want to hear any more lies. I buried the phone under a pillow so I didn't have to hear it. I wanted to go back to sleep and wake up to find it was all a dream, but I knew that wasn't going to happen.

I needed a distraction to take my mind off of things. I remembered TJ telling me to call her if I needed anything, but I didn't want to burden her with this. She'd think I was just some foolish kid.

I thought about how easy Rissa had been to talk to the night before. I dialed her number and waited for her to answer.

"I would love to hang out," she told me. "What room are you in?"

I told her and hung up the phone. Looking in the mirror over the sink, I realized how bad I looked. My eyes were swollen and red. My nose looked like a giant cherry stuck in the middle of my face. I filled my hands with cold water and buried my face in them. I needed to make myself look a little more presentable. It wasn't working. I still looked terrible when I heard the knock. I immediately felt better when I saw Rissa through the tiny hole in the door.

"I thought about taking you out to eat, but judging from the tone of your voice on the phone, I didn't know if you wanted to go out in public. I grabbed some sandwiches and chips from a deli by my place instead."

"I'm so glad you came," I told her as I closed the door behind her. "I really need some company."

"What's wrong? You look awful."

"I had a tough afternoon," I said sitting on the edge of the bed.

"The job interview didn't go well?" she asked.

"The interview went great. I start the job tomorrow. It was everything after that sucked."

"Talk to me," she said as she sat beside me.

I don't know what it was, but something about her demeanor made me so comfortable. I just let everything pour out.

"I went to Randi's when I got out of the interview. I was so excited. I picked up some take out and thought that we could have lunch before she went to work. She wasn't home, but this other chick was. She basically told me to leave Randi alone."

I felt the knot come back into my throat and I tried to push it back down. I didn't want to break down again, especially not in front of Rissa.

"She told me that Randi had moved on and I should do the same. She told me that Randi had said I didn't accept that we had broken up. Randi told me that they were both in the intern program and the studio had put them together as roommates in that apartment. I don't know what to do. I don't know what to believe. I love Randi so much."

I couldn't hold the tears back any longer. I sobbed uncontrollably and Rissa wrapped her arms around me and held me as I cried. Once I had regained my composure, she let me go and forced me to look her in the eyes.

"Faith, sometimes when people are apart they make bad decisions. Randi has been away from you for some time. She obviously couldn't handle the long distance thing. I'm not trying to justify what she's done, but it happens. You can't let this get you down. You have enough to deal with, you know, with starting your life over."

Rissa was amazing. She was only three years older than me, but seemed years older at that moment.

"So," I said to her, changing the subject. "TJ says everyone has a story. You know mine. What's yours?"

Her laugh was a beautiful melody and her smile brightened my spirits.

"I have a bunch of stories. Which one do you want to know?"

"Anything you want to tell me."

"Okay," she said taking a deep breath. "I grew up in New Mexico. My dad is in the military and was stationed there when he met my mom. She was an immigrant from Mexico and she worked as a waitress at a restaurant the he used to go to with his friends. The story was that he fell in love with her at first sight and asked her to marry him on the spot. She thought he was joking and turned him down. He begged her to go out with him, which she finally did. They married three months later and I was born two years after that. My younger brother was born three years after me. My parents never knew I was gay until my little brother got mad at me once and told them. They're Catholic, so that didn't turn out too well. They threw me out of the house and I stayed with different friends, sleeping on their floors and sofas for a while before I decided to come to L.A. to try to break into the music business."

"How old were you?"

"Fifteen."

"Wow. I can't imagine being on my own at that age. I'm having a hard enough time dealing with it now."

The tone of her voice turned more serious as she continued.

"It was hard. I lived on the street for a long time, sleeping wherever I could find a dry place and begging for money. I hooked up with a group of kids that had taken over this abandoned building in one of the industrial areas. They had made quite a nice little place out of it, actually. There wasn't any running water or electricity, but at least it was dry. There were probably twenty of us that lived there. We all pitched in what money we could scrounge up for food. There were some that I was sure stole food from some of the little stores in the area, but I never did. I did get caught up in some other stuff while I was with them."

"Drugs?" I asked.

"Among other things."

Rissa's voice began to shake a little as she talked. I told her that she didn't have to tell me anything that she didn't want to, but she continued.

"One of the girls was out one night and a guy picked her up. She came home with more food than I had seen in months. She kept going out at night and coming back with more money. She asked me to go with her one night and I did."

Her eyes were no longer on me. She nervously picked at the seam on her jeans as she relayed more of her story.

"This really disgusting guy stopped us and offered us a hundred bucks if we would both go with him. I almost backed out, but she talked me into it. She told me to just close my eyes and think of something else. She said that it would be over quick. It wasn't. I was physically ill by the time he finished with us. Then he said that he would give us extra if we would have sex with each other in front of him. I wanted to run screaming, but I wanted the money. It was easy cash and I was desperate."

My heart was breaking for her as she sat there and told me the rest of what happened. I wanted to put my arms around her, but wasn't sure if I should.

"I probably don't have to tell you that it wasn't the only time I did that," she continued. "I eventually got into the drugs to make it easier and things went downhill from there. I just didn't realize how far and fast they were going down."

"Where did you meet TJ?" I interrupted.

"Sasha, the girl that I was telling you about, went out alone one night and disappeared. We never saw her again. I like to tell myself that she met someone and is living happily ever after somewhere, but that's probably far from the truth. Anyway, I had some regular guys that I would see a couple of nights a week, usually in their cars or an alley. Occasionally, I would find someone that would spring for a motel room and I could take a shower. I was leaving a motel one night and took a wrong turn heading back. This group of guys was leaving a bar. They were drunk and started calling out to me. I ignored them and walked as fast as I could to get away from them, but they caught up with me. I was high and couldn't fight them off. There were three of them and they pulled me into an alley."

I noticed that she was crying.

"Rissa, you don't have to do this," I told her as I stroked her arm.

I felt bad for asking her about her past.

"It actually helps me to talk about it," she said, wiping her eyes. "The bricks scratched my face when they pushed me against the wall of the building. I remember feeling the pain and the warm blood as it trickled down my cheek. One of them ripped my skirt off. I felt his rough hands on me and could smell the liquor on his breath. I tried to fight back, but they held me against the wall. All I could do was cry as each one violated me in one way or another. Then there was this blinding pain in the back of my head. My next memory is of TJ sitting beside my hospital bed."

I was crying right along with her. I was glad that she couldn't remember anything else. I don't know if I could have taken listening to more details of what happened to her. It was bad enough to hear what she could remember.

"Apparently one of the guys got scared that I could identify them and he hit me in the head with some kind of metal pipe. The cops found it in the alley. TJ and Pam were the ones that found me all covered in blood and unconscious. They called for help and TJ never left my side until I woke up. They said I was out for over a week. The doctors actually didn't think I was going to make it. They just didn't know how stubborn I am."

It was good to hear the slight laugh come from her after such a horrible story.

"TJ got me into rehab and then set me up with some folks that helped me out when I finished that program. She actually saved my life in more than one way. Once I got clean and on my feet, I started volunteering at the center as a peer counselor for some of the other kids. I was finally able to get a little bit of a start with my music and now things are pretty good."

"Did they ever catch the guys that did that to you?" I asked after a short silence.

"Never did. None of them had fingerprints of DNA in the system. The one thing that really bothers me is the fact that I could pass by them on the street and never know it. I didn't get a good look at them, and even if I did, I was so messed up that I probably wouldn't have remembered them."

"I'm an idiot," I said. "I've been sitting here feeling sorry for myself, and it never crossed my mind that what I am going through is nothing compared to what other people have gone through."

"You're not an idiot," she said putting her hand on mine. "We never know what someone else has been through. Besides, your own hell is based on what you know. Before I came here, a devastating experience for me would've been not getting to go to the mall with my friends."

"I guess so. When I think about it, I've lived a pretty good life, even if I didn't have the greatest parents."

"I have an idea," she said with a sudden sparkle in her eyes. "I work at this club on Friday and Saturday nights. Why don't you go with me tomorrow night?"

My phone rang before I could answer her. I rejected the call as soon as I saw it was Randi.

"That sounds like a great idea," I said.

"It's a date then."

Chapter 4

My first day of work was awesome. Michelle was great while she was getting me settled in and everyone else was very helpful when it came to all of the questions that I had for them. The day flew by and I was headed back to the hotel before I knew it.

Time suddenly slowed once I was in the room. I stared at the clock, waiting on Rissa. I almost jumped out of my skin when I heard the knock on the door.

"Wow! You look amazing," I said when I saw her.

She was dressed in all black. The tight leather vest was very low cut and revealed just a little skin between it and her low-rise pants. I envied girls that had the body and the guts to wear stuff like that. I couldn't do it. I felt terribly self-conscious and underdressed in my jeans and tank top.

"Are you ready?" she asked.

I didn't want her to know just how anxious I had been. Trying to sound casual, I told her I was and we left for the club.

She amazed me as she turned knobs and flipped switches while she worked. She mixed her own music and everyone loved it. She kept the dance floor full all night long.

I had several offers to dance, which I turned down. Rissa tried to get me to loosen up and dance some, but I was happy right there beside her. There was something about her that captivated me, and it wasn't just the fact that she had managed to sneak a drink to me.

Once the club closed and everyone was gone, I helped her load her things into her car and we just drove around the city. It was the first time that I had seen the streets so quiet. They weren't empty by any stretch of the imagination, but things were not as hectic as they were during the day.

Rissa was so energized as we talked. She said that she always felt like that after working a good night at the club. Being able to play music and make people happy was her goal. When she succeeded, it was like a high that she had never experienced before. I wanted to reach a point in my life where I could feel like that instead of the doom that had taken over my thoughts.

I didn't want the night to end and we got back to my hotel way too quickly.

"Would you like to come up for a bit?" I asked her.

"I guess I can," she said as she parked her car. "I don't have anywhere that I have to be at this hour."

"Hey Georgia Girl," Mike called out to me as we walked through the lobby. "Someone came by and left you a message."

I had a sinking feeling in my gut as I took the paper. I didn't open it immediately. I knew who it was from and I just didn't want to ruin a good night. I hadn't taken my phone with me for that very reason.

"Aren't you going to read your message?" Rissa asked as I opened my hotel room door.

"Nope," I answered quickly. "I know it's from Randi and I just can't deal with it right now. I've got to figure out what I'm doing and I can't let her cloud my judgment any more than she already has."

My phone vibrated in the dresser drawer.

"You should probably answer that," Rissa said.

I knew it was Randi before I ever took it out. I silenced it and turned it off.

"If you want to talk with her, I can leave."

"No. I don't want to talk to her right now. I'm still a little…I don't know…hurt…pissed…confused…all of the above."

"I know that feeling," Rissa said with a nervous laugh.

"Anyway," I changed the subject. "I had a great time tonight. It was so interesting watching you do what you love."

"I'm glad you had fun. Maybe we can do it again sometime. Who knows? You might meet someone you like in there sometime, but you'll have to mingle with other people to do it."

"I'm not interested in meeting anyone," I said as I flopped on the bed. "I probably just need to be alone my whole life. It seems like everyone I'm around disappoints me. If I stay alone, there's nobody to do that."

Rissa lay down on the bed beside me and propped on her elbow. Her eyes fixed on mine and I couldn't look away.

"Not everyone is going to do that. You'll meet people that can take the place of those that have hurt you. You just have to let them in. I know it's hard, but if you don't, you'll miss out on a good thing."

I had flashes of the last few days and didn't realize I was crying again until Rissa wiped a tear from my cheek.

"I'm sorry," she apologized. "I sometimes can't keep my mouth in check. I didn't mean to bring that up."

"It's okay. I just had a flashback."

The silence was only disturbed by the sounds of our breathing. I had to close my eyes to break my gaze away from hers. I found myself torn between what I wanted and what I knew was right. It didn't help when I felt her warm soft lips on mine. I should have pushed her away, but I wrapped my arms around her and held her tight. The light scent of her perfume was intoxicating.

"I'm sorry," Rissa said as she pulled away from me.

"Don't be," I whispered. "I think I wanted you to do that."

Rissa stroked my hair and held my gaze, as if she was contemplating her next move. I was breathing heavy and my heart was racing.

In slow motion, I watched her face move closer to mine. Her eyes closed and mine followed. I could feel her warm breath on my skin as her lips touched mine again. My lips parted and I responded to her passionate kiss. She pressed her body into mine.

I felt a tingle inside as she caressed me with her hands. I wanted her to make love to me. I didn't want random sex. I wanted to feel loved and she was well on her way to giving me exactly that.

***

The knock at the door startled both of us.

"Are you expecting someone this morning?" Rissa asked.

"No," I told her as I threw on my t-shirt. "It's probably just someone that has the wrong room. It happens around here several times a day."

The second knock came just as I opened the door. Much to my surprise, it was Randi on the other side of it.

"Faith, I really need to talk to…"

Her sentence trailed off when she saw Rissa still lying in the bed. There was an instant look of hurt in her eyes and I felt horrible. I stood there motionless and unable to speak.

"I guess I can't be mad," she said, shifting her gaze from Rissa back to me. "It's time I came clean with you. I know you talked to Brittany and I need to explain to you exactly what has led up to where we are."

"I can't do it," I said trying to hide the feelings that I had. "I can't listen to more lies from you, Randi. I'm done."

"You two need to talk," Rissa said from behind me. "I'll go so you can."

Before I could stop her, she was out of the bed and in the bathroom with her clothes. Randi and I sat silently until she came back out, fully dressed.

"Call me later," she said as she left. "to let me know you're okay."

"She's beautiful," Randi said when the door closed.

"She certainly is," I said softly. "Look Randi, I…"

"Let me talk," she interrupted me. "I promise. This is the truth this time. I know you're pissed at me and this probably won't change that, but I'd rather you be pissed at me knowing everything."

I sat silently and stared at her as she worked through her thoughts and vocalized them.

"You know I love you, Faith. That hasn't changed at all. The first thing you should know is that there is no internship. I made it all up. I got a little scared when we got so serious back home. I started talking to Brittany online. We got pretty tight, and I decided to come out here for a while. It wasn't because I had feelings for her. I was testing myself, I guess. I needed something to make sure that I was completely ready to commit to you. I thought I would come out here, find a job, stay for a while, and then be able to come back to you. Nothing has worked out that way. I can't find a job and without one, I can't find a place to live on my own. Brittany is completely supporting me right now."

"Just stop." I told her. "Is this supposed to make me feel better? You're telling me that you came all the way out here and shacked up with another woman to make sure you loved me? That has got to be the biggest line of bullshit that I've ever heard. Randi, I love you. I don't need to test myself to know that. I've devoted myself to you since the day we met. I've always been faithful to you, never even looking at another girl, until last night. I think you just need to go."

I had been hurt before, but this whole line that she was feeding me did nothing but infuriate me. I was so mad that I was shaking. I just wanted her gone. I needed time alone to think.

"I do love you, Faith. Don't ever forget that. I hope you can forgive me one day."

I walked her to the door without saying anything else. Just before she walked out, she grabbed me and pulled me to her and kissed me hard on the mouth. One part of me wanted to kiss her back. The other part of me was repulsed that I was that close to falling for her again.

I closed the door behind her and leaned against it. I completely lost control of myself once again. I collapsed and slid down the door. Sitting on the floor, I cried for the longest time.

The ringing of my phone snapped me back. It was probably one of three people. If it was Randi, I couldn't talk to her. I wasn't sure if I wanted to talk to Rissa. I had put her in an uncomfortable position that morning. If it was Cassie, I needed to talk to her. I propelled myself off the floor to answer it.

I was relieved to see my sister's name on my phone. I cleared my throat and tried to sound normal when I answered.

"Are you all right, Faith?" she asked.

"I'm fine," I lied. "How are things there?"

"You don't sound okay. What's going on?"

Cassie might be my younger sister, but she was a lot smarter than most people gave her credit for being. She also knew me like no one else.

"Just a rough couple of days," I told her. "I have a job now though. I'm still trying to get settled into my new surroundings. It's kind of hard when you don't really know anyone."

"Please tell me where you are," she begged.

I debated on whether or not to tell her the truth. I didn't think she would tell our parents, at least I hoped she wouldn't. Even if she did, they would never find me here.

"I'm in California," I finally told her.

"Are you with Randi? How is she? I bet she was glad to see you."

Cassie's sudden excitement was almost more than I could take.

"Randi's fine. I'm not with her though. As a matter of fact…" I paused for a moment before continuing. "I think we're breaking up."

"Why?"

"It's a long story, Cass. I really don't want to get into it right now. How's school?"

"School's okay. If you don't want to talk about Randi, at least tell me about California."

"It is so completely different from home. It's taking me a while to get used to things. I travel almost everywhere by taxi or city bus. There's a lot of traffic and the streets are always busy, unlike back there where everything is closed by dark."

"Have you made any new friends yet?" she asked.

"I've made a couple. I made one on the way out here. She is kind of indirectly responsible for me getting the job, which is really cool. I am the assistant to a senior account executive for an advertising firm. It's pretty interesting."

"Faith, I'll have to call you back later, I hear Mom and Dad moving around. I'm going out to the mall this afternoon with some friends. I'll call you back then."

"Okay, Cass. I love you and miss you."

"I love you too, Sis."

The phone went silent and I sat down on the bed looking at it. Her timing couldn't have been more perfect. That short conversation cheered me up a bit. I wanted to get out and see more of the area. I would have preferred to do it with Rissa, but I guessed that she probably needed some space from me after our awkward morning.

In my explorations, I found a beautiful park. There were a lot of people having picnic lunches with their families and playing with their pets. There was a street vendor on the sidewalk, which was something that I had never seen back home. He had the most delicious smelling sausages and hot dogs. I bought some lunch and found an empty table. A few random dogs came up to check me out. I wasn't sure if it was because of the food or their friendly nature. Either way, the atmosphere did wonders for my mood. On my way back, I reluctantly called Rissa.

"I have been so worried about you," she said as soon as she answered.

"I'm okay," I assured her. "I just needed to clear my head and think for a while. I also thought you might not want to talk to me after this morning."

"Look. I owe you an apology for last night. I think I might have taken advantage of your situation."

"No you didn't," I interrupted her. "I was well aware of what was happening. After this morning, I have no regrets."

"Things didn't go well with Randi?"

"I guess that depends on how you look at it. We talked and she finally told me the truth. Apparently she has lied to me this whole time. I really don't want to get into this on the phone. Are you busy this afternoon?"

"I don't have anything planned until I go to work tonight."

"Why don't you come to the hotel? I'm on my way back there now."

Chapter 5

I accepted Rissa's invitation to go with her to the club that night and had a great time. I even socialized a bit with some other people. Yes, I even danced with a couple of girls. No one could hold my attention like Rissa did though.

The night ended way to early for me and as much as I wanted to spend the night with her again, we both agreed that it would be a bad idea. When she dropped me off at the hotel, I gave her a friendly kiss on the cheek and told her I would call her.

"Hey Georgia Girl," Mike said as I walked through the lobby. "How are things going?"

"Pretty good, I guess. How's Maria?"

"She's good. She asks about you all the time."

"Tell her I said hello. I can't thank y'all enough for all you have done for me. I don't know what I'd have done when I got to town if it hadn't been for y'all."

"We didn't really do anything and you seem to have settled in and made quite a few friends in just the short time that you've been here. You had a visitor while you were out."

"That's just an old friend that I looked up when I got into town."

"It wasn't the same girl that came by before," he said. "This was an older woman. I told her you weren't here and asked if she wanted to leave you a note, but she didn't."

"I think I know who it was," I said. "I'll give her a call in the morning. You have a good night."

I was pretty sure it was TJ, but I wasn't about to call her that late. She would have called or texted me if it was anything important. Besides, I was exhausted.

I had actually slept very little since I'd left home. I think it was finally catching up with me. Once I was in bed, I fell into a deep sleep and didn't move until I was awakened by the pounding on the door. I glanced at the clock and realized it was almost noon.

Before I could get dressed, the person outside the door was pounding again.

"Just a minute!" I called out in an irritated tone.

Thinking that it was the housekeeping staff, I opened the door without looking to see who it was. I was shocked when I saw Brittany standing in front of me. Her eyes were puffy and she looked horrible.

"Is she here with you?" she asked in a shaky voice.

"Who? Randi?"

"Of course. Who else would I be looking for?"

She was trying to look around me so I stepped to the side.

"She's not here. You can come in and look for yourself."

"She left home yesterday to come see you. She hasn't been back since. I assumed you would know where she is."

She walked into the room and looked around. When she didn't fine Randi, she sat down in the chair in the corner.

"She did come by here yesterday and we talked for a while," I said in an irritated tone. "I haven't seen her since I sent her away. Have you tried calling her?"

"She's not answering her cell. The last time I called, it went straight to voicemail."

"I don't know what to tell you," I said. "Maybe she just needs some time to think about things and decide what she is going to do. "

"Things were going really good until you showed up here," she said with resentment.

"If Randi had been honest with me from the beginning, I would've never come. I thought we still had a relationship because she led me to believe that. If there's a problem between the two of you, it isn't my fault. You'll have to take that up with her. Now, if you don't mind, I have things to do."

Brittany took the hint and left. I couldn't believe the nerve she had. Randi would have to do something about that. I wasn't going to have that woman showing up and bothering me because she couldn't keep her little toy in check.

By the time I found my phone and dialed Randi's number I was furious. I had the entire call planned out in my head. I was going to give her a piece of my mind, even if it was just on her voicemail. Imagine my surprise when a strange male voice answered her phone.

"I need to speak with Randi," I curtly said.

"She can't come to the phone at the moment," he told me. "May I ask who this is?"

"Who I am isn't important," I responded. "I just need to speak with her. Put her on the phone please."

"Ma'am, my name is Seth. I'm a nurse at Mercy. She can't speak to you at the moment. Are you a family member?"

I was frozen. The anger had been replaced by a huge lump in my throat. I finally swallowed it and was able to talk again.

"Is Randi all right?"

"We really need to speak with a family member. Are you related to her?" he asked again.

"No," I whispered. "I'm not family. What's happened?"

"I can't give any information to anyone not related to her. Do you know how to get in touch with her family?"

"She doesn't have anyone here," I told the stranger. "I'm the closest thing she has to a relative. Please just tell me if she is all right."

"I'm sorry," he said apologetically. "I can't give you any information. If you can get in touch with a relative, let them know that she is in ICU at Mercy hospital."

I hung up before he could say anything else. I had to get to the hospital, but I didn't want to go alone. I couldn't ask Rissa to go with me. That would put her in another uncomfortable situation. TJ was my only other choice. She didn't hesitate when I called and asked her.

Once we were there, TJ took control of everything. It seemed that she could get any information that she wanted. The nurses quickly told her everything that they knew about the accident.

Apparently Randi was driving along a very curvy road out in the middle of nowhere and lost control of the car. She must have been driving at a high rate speed because the car flipped several times. Someone came along and saw the wreckage and called for help. No one knew exactly how long she had laid out there unconscious.

The doctor that TJ spoke with explained everything that they had done and what could be expected. Randi was in very critical condition. Even though I had been so furious with her earlier, I was terrified for her at that moment. I did love her and didn't want anything bad to happen to her. I was so confused.

"This is my fault," I told TJ once we left the hospital.

"No it's not, Faith."

"Yeah it is, TJ. She came to see me yesterday and I made her leave. I knew she was upset when she left. If I had just…"

"Faith," she interrupted. "You can't blame yourself. Randi put you in a bad position. She made the choices that have led up to this. She chose to cheat on you and lie about it. I'm sorry to say this, but she chose to be flying out there on that highway."

"Do you think I should go see Brittany and tell her?" I asked.

"Randi was driving her car, and like it or not, they are involved. I think I probably would."

"Will you go with me?" I asked, probably sounding pathetic.

"Of course I will."

Things went better at Brittany's than I expected. TJ did most of the talking, explaining what the doctor had said. Brittany was shaken by the news, but thankful that we had told her. I almost felt sorry for her. I wondered if she was feeling the same feelings that I was. After all, Randi had been dishonest with both of us.

As I lay in bed that night, random thoughts ran through my mind and kept me awake. My feelings were a jumbled mess. On one hand, I hated Randi for what she had done to me. On the other, I couldn't help worrying about her as she lay unconscious in that hospital room. Rissa complicated matters even more. I wanted to get to know her better, but it wasn't fair for me to drag her into my crazy, mixed up life. I had to get my own feelings straight before I could move on to another relationship.

Chapter 6

Every day for a week and a half, I spent my lunch break and most of my evenings in Randi's hospital room, waiting for her to wake up. My nights were restless as I tried to figure out exactly what I was going to do. That decision was made for me when she finally awoke.

"Where's Brittany?" she asked.

The nurse obviously saw the look on my face.

"She's heavily medicated," she said to me. "I'm sure she's a little confused."

"Probably," I said as calmly as I could.

After the nurse left, I walked to the side of the bed and looked at Randi. Her face was still slightly swollen and the bruises were starting to yellow.

"How bad are you hurting?" I asked.

"I'm pretty sore. Do you know what happened?"

"You totaled Brittany's car and almost killed yourself."

"Does she know where I am?"

"She does. She's been every day. Do you remember anything that happened?"

"A little. I know I was driving and hit something on the road. I lost control. I don't remember anything else. How did y'all find out where I was?"

"I called your phone and a nurse answered it. He wouldn't tell me anything other than you was in the hospital. I got someone to bring me here. Once I saw you and knew that you were alive, I let Brittany know."

"I bet she's pissed that I fucked up her car."

"You know Randi, she didn't even mention the car to me. She was more concerned about you. As a matter of fact, she showed up at my hotel before we even knew you were here. She was worried that you hadn't come home. She cares about you. Now that you're awake and apparently going to be okay, I'm sure she'll be thrilled. If you'll give me her number, I'll call her and tell her. I really don't want to go back to that apartment and see her."

"I'm sorry, Faith."

"Don't be. Obviously we weren't meant to be together. You've got someone that cares about you. Enjoy that."

"I've hurt you though."

"I'll be all right," I bravely said.

I couldn't keep the fake façade up much longer. Telling her good bye and getting out of there before I broke down was hard, but necessary. I knew deep down inside that it would be the last time I saw her, unless by accident. That was the way it was going to have to be though.

***

The television played in the background as I sat in the middle of the hotel bed. I had lived a lifetime of devastation in the last couple of weeks. It was taking a toll on me. I felt like I needed to go somewhere else and start all over again, even though I hadn't even gotten a good start here. Like home, there were bad memories and I didn't even want to be in the same town as Randi, even though it was unlikely that we would ever run into each other.

I had no idea where I would go. I sat and wondered if TJ could help. Maybe she had connections somewhere else and could give me some ideas. I was about to dial her number when the knock at the door stopped me.

I contemplated not answering because I really wasn't in the mood to see anyone. The second knock was more persistent so I got up and walked slowly to the door.

"It's about time you answered," Rissa said with a huge smile when I finally opened the door.

"Hey. Come on in."

"You look terrible," she said after she kissed me on the cheek.

"Thanks. I feel terrible," I told her with a sarcastic laugh.

"I know you needed some time, but I wanted to make sure you were all right. I started to call, but decided to come see for myself."

"I'll be all right, eventually. I just have a lot to sort through right now," I told her.

"I know I don't need to add to that," she said seriously. "I have missed you though."

"I'm actually glad you came," I told her. "I really need a friend right now."

"I can be that," she said. "Talk to me. How is Randi?"

"She's going to be fine. She woke up and asked for Brittany immediately."

"That sucks."

"It hurt, but I kept my cool. I told her I was okay with things and she should be thankful that she had Brittany. I was proud of myself for keeping it together."

"Are you sure you want it to be over?" she asked.

I thought for a brief moment before answering.

"Not really, but it has to be. She made a choice and I have to accept that. I just need to move on without her. I just don't know where to go from here."

"You're not thinking about leaving L.A. are you?"

"Actually, I am. I came here solely to be with her. I really don't have any connection to this town. I've even considered going back home. If I'm not seeing Randi, there wouldn't be a problem there."

"What about when you find someone else?" she asked. "Don't you think the same thing will happen all over again?"

She was right. Unless I planned to spend the rest of my life alone, I could never go back to Georgia.

"I'll tell you what," Rissa said. "Let me take you out to dinner and we can talk through everything and see what kind of options you really have. I know from experience that we don't always think clearly when we're hurting. It helps to be able to talk it through with someone and get a clear picture of everything. That way you don't end up doing something you'll regret later."

Rissa was right again. If I had thought about things thoroughly, I probably wouldn't be in Los Angeles, but I also wouldn't know the truth about Randi. Dinner wasn't going to hurt anything.

***

"Are you sure you have to go home?" I asked.

She put her arms around me and pulled me close.

"Let's take this a little more slowly," she said looking into my eyes. "I want you to be sure and not jump into something on the rebound."

She kissed me lightly on the lips and left. I stared at the door as it closed behind her. As much I didn't want to admit it, Rissa was right. I didn't need to jump into something serious right away.

I felt a little better after the evening with her, but still not well enough to get a good night's sleep. My restlessness wasn't helped by all the city sounds throughout the night. Sirens, people on the street and in the hall, and the car horns couldn't even be silenced when I put my pillow over my head. I tossed and turned until the light streamed through the gap in the curtains.

I was too exhausted to go to work. Even though I had only been there a couple of weeks and I knew it would look bad, I called Michelle and told her I was sick. I crawled back in bed and hugged my pillow tightly.

I had just drifted off to sleep when my phone rang. It was Cassie's number. I assumed something was wrong if she was calling me this time of day. She should have been in school. The nausea flooded in when I heard my mother's voice on the other end.

"Faith, where are you?"

I should have hung up immediately, but couldn't.

"Faith? Are you there?"

"Are you going through Cassie's things now?"

The animosity and disgust filled my voice.

"Where are you? We're worried about you."

"Really? You're so worried that you don't even try to call me for weeks?"

"I knew if I called, you wouldn't answer. Cassie dropped her phone on the way out to school this morning. I figured you would answer her number, especially when I saw that she had been in contact with you."

"So y'all are invading her privacy too? You don't have to do that. She's a good girl. She won't disappoint you like I did."

"Faith, you haven't disappointed us. We just want to help you."

"I don't need help. There is absolutely nothing wrong with me."

"Who are you staying with? We'll come get you."

"I'm not staying with anyone," I told her. "I don't need anyone to come get me. You two made it clear how you felt about me so you can forget I exist. It'll make your life easier if you don't have the embarrassment of having someone like me as a daughter. You can keep up your perfect appearance."

"Faith…"

I hung up before she could say anything else. My heart was pounding in my ears and my entire body was shaking. I wondered how easy it would be to go back and pretend that everything was all right. Could I do it? Could I stand living a fake life for the benefit of everyone else? I was flooded with nausea at the thought.

Chapter 7

It amazed me how fast a seemingly perfect life could fall apart in a matter of a few days. I had gone from living the life of a middle class college student with a wonderful girlfriend to living in a hotel room in a strange city and finding out that my girlfriend wasn't what she had seemed. I had a job, and for that I was thankful, but it barely paid for my room and food. Was this how I wanted to spend the rest of my life?

I had no other options though. I knew I couldn't go home. Even if I had the money to do so, I couldn't go back to that life. The more I thought about it, the more I realized that part of my existence was closed to me.

When I looked around, I realized that I had no clue where I was. I had been walking and thinking for hours, not paying any attention to where I was going. I was in a part of the city that I hadn't ever seen. It appeared to be mostly residential, with a few small stores here and there. The buildings were run down and most had bars on the windows. People strolled along the sidewalks, as if they had no particular place to go. A few stared at me like they knew I didn't belong there. I was very uncomfortable.

It was getting dark and I hadn't seen a cab for quite some time. I started looking for landmarks to try and find my way out of whatever neighborhood I was in. I stopped in a small store and bought a drink, hoping that I could get directions from the man working there. He wasn't any help at all. He lived in the neighborhood and didn't know where anything was outside of it.

The later it got, the more nervous I became. I walked block after block, but I still didn't find anything familiar. I had taken my phone out of my pocket to try to call TJ or Rissa to see if they could come get me when a guy bumped into me. He seemed oblivious to the fact that he knocked me against the wall. I noticed a group of younger teenage boys watching me as I regained my balance. They started toward me and I took off in almost a run down the sidewalk.

All of the stores in the next few blocks had closed. There was nowhere that I could duck into for safety. I couldn't seem to shake the group of boys. My heart was pounding so hard. I thought it was going to pop out of my chest.

"Hey!" one of the guys in the group called out to me.

I started to run faster. I thought about the story that Rissa had told me about the night she was attacked. My chest was hurting from my heavy breathing. The guy was closing the gap behind me and I couldn't go any faster.

"Shit!" I exclaimed when I reached for my phone in my pocket.

I was holding it when the guy bumped me. I must have dropped it. I knew I was screwed then because I couldn't even call for help.

I felt a cold chill run down my spine as the guy chasing me grabbed my arm. I almost lost my balance again from the abrupt stop. I turned to look at him. I figured if I survived whatever was about to happen to me, I could at least give a description of him. He must have seen the fear in my eyes.

"You dropped your phone back there when that old dude ran into you," he said.

I looked down and saw it in his outstretched hand. I was shaking so bad when I reached for it. Getting words out of my mouth was difficult.

"Thanks," I finally managed.

"You're welcome. Damn girl. You're fast. I was about to give up on catching you."

"I'm sorry. I thought…"

I couldn't finish that sentence. This guy was doing me a favor. I couldn't tell him what I thought was about to happen to me.

"Do you know where I can find a cab around here?" I asked.

"You won't get one here after dark. They refuse to come down here. Where are you trying to get to?"

I was still a little unsettled and didn't want to tell him where I was actually going. Thinking quickly, I told him that I wanted to get to Tony's. If I could get to the diner, I could find my way back to the hotel.

"Wow. You're a long way from there," he said. "I'll walk with you until you find a cab. It really isn't a good idea for you to walk around here after dark alone anyway. There are some crazy people on the streets down here."

We were silent as he walked with me for several blocks. There was an obvious change in the neighborhoods. Everything was better kept and better lit. I finally saw a cab and flagged it down. Before I got in, I thanked him for helping me and apologized again for misinterpreting his intentions.

"Where to?" the driver asked when I closed the door.

I gave him the address of the hotel instead of the diner and settled back in the seat for the ride. I finally got my breathing under control and relaxed a little.

***

My heart leapt when I saw Rissa sitting in the lobby. Her long black hair flowed down her shoulders as she flipped through one of the old magazines that were kept there. She didn't even notice me until I spoke to her.

"I am so glad to see you here," I said as I hugged her.

"Really? I was afraid that you wouldn't want any company."

"Not at all," I told her when I finally let her go.

My senses were so much more alive around her than they had been in the past. I noticed her perfume filling the elevator as we quietly rode up to my floor. I could hear the sounds of her even breathing.

"How are you feeling?" she asked once we were alone.

"Better," I told her. "I've spent a lot of time thinking. I think I finally have things straight in my head."

"That's good. Are you sure you're all right? You look like you've had a rough day." she asked, seeming very concerned.

"Yeah. I'm glad to be back here though. I got a little lost today," I told her as we sat on the edge of the bed.

I gave her details of my walk, including my scare with the group of guys. She hugged me tightly, trying to soothe me.

"Please don't ever take off like that again. Anything could have happened to you," she said.

Rissa touched my arm tenderly. The heat from her skin sent tingles through me. I looked into her dark brown eyes as she sat still and quiet on the bed. Leaning over, I kissed her gently on the lips.

"Are you sure about this?" she asked in a whisper.

"Very sure," I whispered back to her.

Chapter 8

"This is the last box," I said as I packed it in the trunk of Rissa's small car.

"I guess it's a good thing you haven't had time to collect much stuff since you've been here," she teased.

"I guess so. Let me go check the room once more, turn in the key, and I'll be ready to go."

I took one last look around the empty hotel room that had been home for the past several months. I was actually going to miss it a little, but not enough to turn down Rissa's offer to move in with her. We had an agreement that we would start out as roommates and I was going to carry my share of the bills. We could see how our relationship developed before we thought of ourselves as a couple.

I gave Mike a hug and thanked him again for everything that he and Maria had done for me.

"You know you can always come back and visit," he told me. "I don't plan on going anywhere any time soon, and Maria just became the night shift manager at the diner. She isn't going to give that up. Promise to come see us?"

"I will," I told him, even though I thought in the back of my mind of how people always say they'll keep in touch and never do.

I hadn't heard from Randi in several weeks, which was a good thing. I was opening a new chapter of my life and I didn't want her playing a part in it. I was concerned about how she was doing in her recovery from the accident, but I couldn't make myself call her to find out. I guessed that I would always have some feelings for her, but I didn't think I would ever love her again the way that I had.

Thankfully, my mother hadn't called again either. I had talked to Cassie several times. She called pretending to need advice a couple of times, but I knew she just wanted to talk. I missed talking with her every day and wished that I could be closer to her, but that couldn't happen. She didn't let Mom or Dad know about it, but she was planning to apply to colleges in California. We could be together then, but the phone would have to be our connection for now.

"You look like you're in deep thought," Rissa said as she maneuvered her car through the busy streets.

"I guess I was."

"You want to talk about it?"

I looked at her and smiled.

"It's nothing serious. I was just thinking about how things have changed. How I thought my life was over when I first got here and now things are looking so much better. I think I owe a lot to you and TJ. Y'all have done so much for me."

"You might owe TJ a little, but you don't owe me anything. I think I was an innocent bystander that got sucked into TJ's matchmaking web."

"Do you think that's what she was doing when she introduced us?" I asked.

"Of course it was. She's notorious for trying to hook people up. She does a pretty good job of it most of the time.

"Do you think she did a good job this time?"

"I guess," Rissa teased. "Once we see how our relationship will go, then I'll give you a definite answer to that."

***

"I'm sorry," Rissa apologized as she opened the bedroom door. "This room has been my studio for quite some time and I haven't had a chance to get all of my equipment out of it yet. I'm not sure where to put it all."

"It's okay," I assured her. "It isn't like I have a lot of stuff to fill the room. You can leave it."

"I'll get it as soon as I can. I work a lot when I'm home and you might want your privacy."

"It's really okay. I'm kind of used to being in a cramped space," I said half joking. "I actually have room to move around here as opposed to that hotel room."

"You have plenty of closet space here," Rissa said opening the walk-in closet so that I could see it. "If you need more, there is another closet in the hall beside the bathroom. I have a dresser in storage that we can bring up for you. What else do you need?"

"I can't think of anything else," I told her. "This is actually perfect."

We talked and laughed while I unpacked my things and put them away. It felt good to have a permanent place to stay, but it felt even better knowing that Rissa was there with me. I have to admit, the first time I was with Rissa was out of revenge for what Randi had done to me, but I had fallen hard for her. I wasn't sure if I was actually in love with her, but I was definitely close.

Once I had everything unpacked and the boxes disposed of, we settled down on the sofa in the living room to rest.

"I almost forgot," Rissa said with a smile. "I have a job interview tomorrow."

"Really? Are you thinking about leaving the club?"

"No. This is a real day job. A musician friend of mine has been talking about me to the manager of a recording studio. He wants to talk to me about a job that he has opening up."

"That would be awesome," I told her. "If you could get your foot in the door with a studio, you could really go somewhere with your own music."

"I know. I am pretty excited about it. Besides, if it works out, I could give up the gig at the club in the future and we would work roughly the same hours. It'll give us more time together."

I leaned on Rissa's shoulder and she put her arm around me and held me tightly.

"That will be good," I said looking up at her.

I closed my eyes and thought about how comfortable I was. I don't mean just physically comfortable, but emotionally comfortable. With all of turmoil that I had gone through, Rissa had been a stabilizing force. Her emotional strength had been a model for me to follow. She had given me motivation to find my own inner strength.

Chapter 9

"Rissa, I'm home."

The apartment was dark and silent. She was usually home before me, but anything could have kept her late. Her new job had become very demanding and she put in a lot of hours at the studio. I plundered through the kitchen for a snack and settled onto the sofa to watch television and wait for her. I must've been more tired than I thought because my eyes grew heavy and the sound of the television became muffled before it faded into nothingness.

Rissa's warm soft lips touched mine gently and I slowly opened my eyes. I couldn't have been awakened any better. Her beauty still amazed me.

"Hey," I said in a sleepy voice. "I'm sorry. I must have fallen asleep waiting on you."

"It's okay," she smiled at me as she got up from the floor. "I am a lot later than I expected to be tonight. I should have called"

"If I had known what time you would he home, I could have made dinner," I told her as I sat up on the sofa.

"I'm taking you out to dinner tonight to celebrate," she told me.

"What are we celebrating?" I asked feeling a little puzzled.

"I'll tell you at the restaurant. We have reservations in an hour."

"I better get changed then. Where are we going?"

"It's a surprise," she said as a devious smile crossed her face.

"Well, how should I dress?"

"Just wear that pretty little black dress and you'll be fine," she told me.

***

"How long before you let me in on what's going on?" I asked as the waiter brought our drinks and appetizer.

Rissa looked serious as she took my hand.

"I know that you said you wanted to take things slow with us, and that's fine. Personally, I think things are going really well. What do you think?"

"I think it's good," I said apprehensively.

"Okay. I'll get right to the point. Dino came in today and was talking to me about how things are going at the studio. He's really pleased with my work, and he made me an offer for something different. I just need to talk to you before I give him an answer."

I had a sudden sinking feeling in the pit of my stomach. I wasn't sure what was coming next and I didn't know if I was ready for whatever it was. I finally had a normal life and I wanted it to stay that way. I had this feeling that whatever she was about to say was going to disrupt everything.

"You don't need my opinion on your job," I told her and pulled my hand away from hers.

"Actually, I do on this," she replied. "Dino wants me to go to the New York studio."

That was the moment that my heart hit the bottom of my stomach. I knew Rissa wouldn't pass up an opportunity to go to New York. I wouldn't have either. I also knew that once she got there, she would find someone a lot better than me. Our relationship was just about to be over.

"That's great," I tried to sound excited. "How long will you be gone?"

"That's the thing," she said with a pause. "It's permanent."

"Wow. I didn't expect that."

The lump in my throat was huge, but I was able to swallow it and continue.

"I guess I'll need to start looking for another apartment. When will you be leaving?"

"That's the other huge part of this discussion."

Rissa moved her chair around to beside me and took my hand from my lap.

"I want you to come with me," she said. "I know it's not what we've talked about as far as our relationship goes, but I don't want to go without you, Faith. I have been crazy about you from day one. I thought I was going to lose you when Randi had her accident. It almost killed me being away from you, but you needed that time. I really don't want to be away from you ever again. That is, if you're willing to do this."

I sat completely speechless and tried to digest what Rissa had just asked me. The seconds ticked by so slowly that it seemed like time had stopped. Everyone in the restaurant disappeared except for us.

"I understand if you need some time to think about it."

Rissa's voice brought me back and the room came back to life.

"No," I said. "I don't have to think about it. If that's what you want, I'm with you."

I'm pretty sure the huge smile on my face was goofy looking, but I was thrilled.

"No reservations?" she asked.

"Only a couple," I confessed. "The main thing is my job and my financial situation. That move will be expensive. I don't know that I can afford it."

"I've been thinking about that too," Rissa said as she moved her chair back to its original spot at the table. "I'm getting a huge raise to take this job and they're setting us up in an apartment that the studio owns. That means no rent for us. They're even offering to pay all of our moving expenses just to get me up there. Money isn't really going to be an issue."

"Let's do it then," I said with excitement.

"Are you sure?"

"If it's what you want, I'm game. I have nothing to lose here. It isn't like I have family to worry about. I think it'll be exciting. When do they want you to go?"

"Dino wants me to go as soon as possible. He said he could give me a couple of weeks to get things packed and ready. I guess you need to turn in your resignation at work tomorrow."

Chapter 10

"Are you sure you don't mind this?" I asked Rissa as I was getting dressed.

"I don't," she told me. "I honestly think you need to do it. It'll be good for both of you."

"You know you can go with me if you want," I told her.

"It's better if I stay out of it," Rissa said as she wrapped her arms around me. "You two can talk openly and you can get some sort of closure."

"I promise I won't be gone long."

"Take as long as you need. I have plenty to do to keep me occupied while you're gone."

Rissa had to be the most understanding person in the world. I doubted that I could have sat home calmly while she went to meet an ex. I guess she knew that she didn't have anything to worry about. Plus, she was right. This was a final good-bye for Randi and me.

Randi and I agreed to meet at Tony's. It was familiar to both of us and very public. I got there first, as usual. I ordered a cup of coffee to settle my nerves. It had just arrived when I saw Randi come through the door on her crutches.

"I didn't realize you were still in a cast," I said as she sat down.

"It comes off tomorrow," she said while she wrangled the crutches into the booth and out of the way. "I can't wait. Of all the injuries, my leg was the hardest to heal and the hardest to deal with."

"How are you doing since the accident?"

I was concerned for her well-being. It wasn't concern out of the love I once felt, but it was genuine.

"I still have some headaches, but the doctor says they'll go away eventually. They are becoming less frequent and less severe. My shoulder was pretty messed up for a while, but it is better now. It's just my leg. They had to put a rod in it because it was shattered. I'll probably have a permanent limp."

"I'm sorry."

"Don't be," she told me. "None of this was your fault. It was all mine. I have made some pretty bad decisions and I'm paying for them now."

"How are things with you and Brittany?"

"It's been tense, but she has done a phenomenal job of taking care of me. What about you? How are things going for you?"

"That's kind of why I wanted to meet you today. I have a couple of things to tell you."

The waitress came back to refill my coffee and Randi ordered a cup for herself.

"I moved in with Rissa a while back," I began. "We have gotten pretty serious since."

"Does she treat you good?" Randi asked.

"Yeah. She's really great."

My gaze was focused on the table. I couldn't look Randi in the eyes because I was afraid that I would see hurt in them.

"I'm leaving tomorrow," I finally said after working up the courage.

"Are you going back home?"

"I am going back east, but not home. Rissa's being transferred with her job and she wants me to go with her. We have everything packed and ready to go, but I had to see you one last time. I guess to tie up any loose ends that we might have."

"That's great," Randi said, trying to sound happy. "I hope things work out for you. Where are y'all going?"

"New York."

"Wow. Are you ready for that?"

"I am. I can't wait, actually."

"I'm happy for you, Faith. I know I've put you through hell the last few months. I don't expect you to ever be able to forgive me completely, but I do want you to know that I love you."

I opened my mouth to speak, but Randi cut me off.

"I'm not trying to get you back. I know that part of our lives is over. I just want you to know how sorry I am for everything. I screwed up and lost you. I just hope that Rissa realizes how lucky she is to have you. I didn't realize that until it was too late."

"Randi, it has been rough," I confessed to her. "I had huge dreams when I came here. We all know they didn't come true, but things have a way of working out for the best. It may not seem like we're better off at first, but in the end, we are."

We talked for quite a while, just like old friends would do. It was nice to be able to do that with her without that cloud of deception hanging over us.

"I've got to go," I said after I glanced at my watch. "We still have quite a bit to do before tomorrow."

"It was great to see you. I'm glad you called me to let me know."

Randi pulled herself to her feet and grabbed her crutches. I gently hugged her while she rested her weight on them.

"Take care of yourself, Randi."

I gently kissed her on the cheek and broke the embrace. Surprisingly, I didn't feel any remorse. Instead, I felt a giant weight lift off of my mind and heart.

"You too," she said quietly.

***

I was absolutely giddy as we watched the movers load everything onto the truck. The last few days had been crazy with us trying to get everything packed and making final arrangements, but we managed to get it all done. All we had left to do was stop by the studio and pick up the keys to the apartment in New York.

"I never thought I would head back east," I told Rissa once we were on the highway. "I thought that once I got settled out here that was it."

"Are you having regrets?" she asked.

"None at all," I told her as I grabbed her free hand. "It's just another open door and I am ready to explore what's on the other side of it. More importantly, I am ready to explore it with you."

She squeezed my hand tightly and I felt a wave of comfort flow over me. It was a feeling that had been foreign to me for way too long. At that moment I knew that I was where I was supposed to be. I had been filled with doubts about my decisions over the last few months, but this was one that I was one hundred percent sure about. I closed my eyes and leaned back in the seat, listening to the hum of the tires on the road.

***

I opened my eyes and looked around. I felt a bit confused as I saw the sign welcoming us to Georgia. I knew that Rissa had checked the map, but I thought there would be a much shorter route than through my home state.

"Why are we going through Georgia?" I asked.

Rissa smiled that beautiful smile of hers and laughed slightly.

"I wanted to see if the entire state was as charming and beautiful as you."

"Trust me, it isn't all that great. It certainly isn't what you're used to. How much longer are you going to drive tonight before we stop?"

"Not much longer. I guess I should go ahead and fill you in on something."

I looked at her suspiciously, but didn't say anything.

"I called your sister a few days ago. She knows we're coming through on our way and she's going to be waiting on us at the hotel I reserved. I thought you would enjoy seeing her, since it's been a while."

"Are you serious?" I exclaimed.

"Completely. I texted her a little while ago and she has everything arranged. Your parents think she is spending the night with a friend, but that friend is actually picking her up so she can meet us."

I couldn't believe it. Once again, Rissa had proven just how wonderful she was. The one thing that I wanted most was to see Cassie again. Now it was happening.

"I hope she's careful. The last thing I want is for my parents to show up and cause a scene. I really don't want you involved in that," I told Rissa.

The night turned out more wonderful than I could have imagined. I should have slept, but we spent the entire night talking. It was just like a lot of nights when I was home. I hated to leave that next morning, but Rissa and I had to get back on the road. At least now I would be much closer to Cassie than before. Things really were looking up for me.